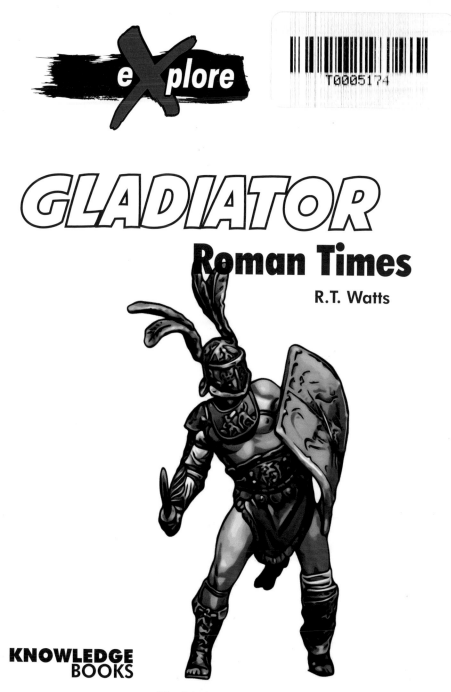

eXplore

T0005174

GLADIATOR
Roman Times

R.T. Watts

KNOWLEDGE BOOKS

© Knowledge Books and Software

Teacher Notes:

Gladiators trained fiercely and often fought to the death and were a vitally important tool for the Emperor to help keep the people happy. Read about the many and varied skills of Rome's gladiators and their amazing and deadly weapons of choice. Further opportunities are available to discuss the issue of slavery and the impact on exotic animal populations.

Discussion points for consideration:

1. Gladiators were like Roman celebrities. Why do you think they were so important to the people and the emperor?

2. Discuss the pros and cons of the different types of armour and weapons used by each of the gladiators in the story.

3. Exotic animal numbers were decimated during this time. Discuss the impact of this and how things are different today.

Sight words, difficult to decode words, and infrequent words to be introduced and practiced before reading this book:

Equites, Thracians, Colosseum, aqueducts, gladiators, citizens, incredibly, extreme, chariots, trident, Caligula, Spartacus, gladiatrix, equipment, unbelievable, disappeared, engineers, Secutor, successful, emperor, prisoners, Retiarius.

Contents

1. About the Roman Empire

2. Aqueducts

3. Roman Armies

4. Emperors of the Roman Empire

5. Roman Cities

6. Who Were the Gladiators?

7. The Colosseum

8. The End of the Roman Empire

1. About the Roman Empire

Gladiator combat was a popular sport during the Roman Empire. Gladiators fought in the arena and could easily be killed. The gladiators fought other gladiators and animals. People loved seeing gladiators fight.

Who were the Romans? What did they do? Why were they so powerful? How did the Empire last for so long? These are questions people continue to study.

The Roman Empire was run by the Emperor, who fiercely controlled the entire Empire. The Emperor was believed to be a god, who ruled with his special powers. Saying anything bad about the Emperor was a quick way of being fed to wild animals.

The Roman Empire started in Rome. The Empire was run from Rome, and lasted for over 1,000 years. It spread from Rome to North Africa, across Europe, and into parts of the Arab and Persian worlds. It was a mighty empire with strong armies, smart engineers and careful control over the people.

It was very successful for a very long time. The Roman Empire was successful because it brought a certain way of life to the local people. Before the Romans came through, an area would be made up of smaller groups and kingdoms. It was easy to beat up the locals as they had small armies. The Romans then gave the locals a piece of the action. Rome was colonising other countries like France, Spain and Britain.

THE ROMAN EMPIRE

The Romans took over the south of Britain. The Roman army was made up of soldiers from all over Europe. The local people were given control over their area. Local people were given power if they were loyal to Rome.

Roman rule stopped all the rabble and fights. After a hundred years people knew no other life.

The Roman Empire lasted for about 500 years in Britain. It was a long time, and meant that the people did not know any other life.

Roads, bridges and buildings were built around towns. Britain was becoming a country rather than a lot of little kingdoms.

People all over Europe became part of the Roman Empire. The local people could become citizens of Rome if they were good and did a lot to help the Roman Empire.

All of these countries still have Roman buildings and roads. They may be very old, but parts of them still exist. They built strong roads of large cut stones. Soldiers, carts, horses and people could travel along these roads. They did not get muddy or flood – you could travel along these roads at any time. These stone roads were built wide enough for an army to march along. These roads with marble markers are still there to be seen.

2. Aqueducts

Roman towns needed water. How do you get water to flow over 35 miles along a channel? It must flow at a steady rate to supply all the people in town with water. It was open to the air and sunlight which kept the water fresh, clean, and full of air.

These aqueducts are still working today, bringing water from lakes and dams. These were amazing structures which were incredibly precise. If the water went too fast there would be too much water in the town. It had to be just right.

These aqueducts carried water a long way, across valleys and through hills.

3. Roman Armies

Roman soldiers were not gladiators. This would be like comparing baseball players to soldiers today.

Roman soldiers often spent many years in other countries. The Roman Empire was spread over many countries and places.

Local people became soldiers and were trained to work as part of the army.

The Roman army was very large and could easily fight against most other armies. It was not only the largest army, but also the best. They had great weapons and smart ways of fighting.

4. Emperors of the Roman Empire

Roman people believed their emperors were gods. The Emperor of Rome was born into this position. They were like British royalty today.

The emperors took over from the kings of Rome. There are many marble statues of the emperors, which shows how important they were.

The emperor had to stay popular with the people. If the people stopped liking the emperor, then it was time for a change. The people had no power but could stop believing in the emperor and so cause Rome to collapse.

5. Roman Cities

Roman cities were built across the empire. There are places in North Africa today where Roman buildings still stand.

In Jordan and Syria in the Middle East, there are amazing Roman cities. Stone blocks were carved to make buildings.

At the end of the Roman Empire, many of these buildings became ruins. Local people took the stone to build houses. Some of the stone was used for roads.

Today, there are still Roman buildings in many parts of the empire. These are still standing after 2000 years.

6. Who Were the Gladiators?

In movies, it is often shown that gladiators were slaves. Some gladiators were forced to come to the arena as slaves. It was a very scary thing to have happen. You get dragged along to fight a gladiator. Someone was going to get hurt and maybe killed.

Gladiator fighting was very popular. It was not all criminals, prisoners and slaves who fought. Some men thought gladiator combat was like an extreme sport. They wanted to be gladiators to make money and become famous.

There was not just one type of gladiator. There were all sorts of armour and ways of fighting.

There were many forms, or classes, of gladiators.

There would be rules as to what you could do with each type of sword and armour.

Some of the gladiators rode horses or chariots. Others carried giant forks and nets. Special gladiators just fought animals.

This video gives an intro to the types of gladiators and is well worth reviewing.

MAPΓAPEITHC   EΛΛHNIKOC

21

The Retiarius Gladiator. This gladiator had no armour or large sword. This type of gladiator had a large net, a little dagger, and a long fork called a trident. If he trapped his enemy in the net, he could then kill the enemy with his dagger.

This type of gladiator had to move fast, and be quick to jab. These gladiators fought other gladiators and animals. They were not rock star type gladiators. They were thought of as low types, but then got popular again.

If they were good, they were still very dangerous and could easily kill the other gladiators.

The Secutor Gladiator. This gladiator wore heavy armour. The helmet only had tiny peep holes to see out. He carried a large shield and had a massive sword.

These gladiators were used to fight Retiarius gladiators with the nets. They had a big contest and it was a very popular show.

The Secutor would have to attack first. Big rocks were dropped from above and he had to be careful to dodge them. After this he still had to be careful. If he got caught in the net, he was a goner.

The Equites Gladiator. This gladiator rode a horse. He had a helmet over his face and light armour. He carried a short sword. Sometimes he could have a long spear.

This gladiator's sword was short and he could fight on or off his horse. An Equites gladiator would fight other Equites gladiators in the arena.

In the arena, they would fight other Equites while on the horse, or on the ground.

This was a favourite event for the crowd, and this was one of the first battles shown at the start of the games.

The Thracian Gladiators. This gladiator was very popular. He had a round shield, curved blade sword and a wide helmet.

These were popular with some emperors. Emperor Caligula liked the Thracian gladiators and trained himself to fight as a Thracian gladiator.

The story of Spartacus is about a slave who became a Thracian gladiator. He built his own army to attack the Roman army.

29

The Gladiatrix. Women also became gladiators. They were called the Gladiatrices.

The women would wear very little armour. They would be bare-chested and carried a shield with a sword. They would sometimes wear a helmet.

The women would fight each other or wild animals. To be a gladiator required training and permission from the emperor to fight in the arena.

The Gladiatrix was not common but can be seen in wall carvings. The emperor banned women gladiators in about AD 200. Scan the QR code on the next page for more information on women gladiators.

7. The Colosseum

The Colosseum was built for games. Gladiator games and battles were very popular. These were extreme sports and got everyone interested. The gladiator games were stopped for a long time, but Emperor Caligula brought them back. The rest of the emperors saw how popular these fights and games were, and did not stop them.

Gladiators were graded, like in footy games. Your grade was based on your success. The top grade gladiators were the most popular fights.

The Colosseum was opened to show these games.

Believe it or not, there were people to make sure rules were kept for the games. These were the referees. The gladiators were not killed on purpose. They could get hit and die, but it was also an act most of the time. This was like wrestling you see today; it is a lot of fun and drama.

The gladiators were like sumo wrestlers. They spent a lot of time training. A lot of money was spent on their equipment. If they got killed it was a big loss money-wise too! It was a very deadly sport and you did not last a long time.

Watch more on these QR scans here.

Gladiators also fought wild animals in these games. Special gladiator types would only fight wild animals.

These were special gladiators who would fight crocodiles, tigers, bears, elephants and other big animals.

The number of poor animals killed for fun was unbelievable. Some arena games killed thousands of these wild animals.

North Africa's animals nearly disappeared because of these games. Most of the bears and wolves of Europe were killed during this period. It was a mass killing for fun in the arenas.

Some of Rome's emperors fancied they were very good as gladiators too!

Some emperors went into the arena to fight animals and gladiators.
Emperors Caligula, Titus, and Hadrian all had a go.

These emperors wanted some of the glory of being a gladiator. They hoped to become popular with the people.

These were rigged fights. The poor gladiators who had to fight had blunt knives. Or the animals were lame and injured. The emperors made sure they always won so they would look good.

Gladiators were popular like rock stars today. These fighters were famous. The Roman people knew who the best gladiators were. This was a scary sport and you had to be tops to survive.

Gladiators were shown on walls of buildings. The portrait of your favourite gladiator would hang in your room. People would go along to the arena if they knew their favourite gladiator was fighting.

Children would play gladiator sports with fake swords. They would make clay toys of gladiators.

8. The End of the Roman Empire

The Romans had it good for too long
and became weak. The Emperors
built beautiful temples and palaces.
The idea was to have a good time,
and everyone thought things would
never change. The Emperors were not
thinking about the dangers. Enemy
countries were growing stronger. The
Empire went to sleep and let others
slowly take control.

The Roman Empire was split into two
empires. The West was all of Europe
and Britain. The East was Greece,
Hungary, Turkey and a lot of the
Middle East. The centre for the East
was Constantinople. The Roman
Empire in the East went for another
1000 years after the collapse in
Europe in 400 AD.

After 500 years of Roman rule, the Britons were under attack from the Saxons. These were tribes from the north of Europe. The Britons wrote to the Emperor of Rome for help to stop the Saxons. The Roman Emperor no longer had the armies to help.

This was the end of the Roman Empire in Britain as it was invaded from the north. Those 500 years of life as part of the Roman Empire is still present today. Many of the city streets were Roman roads. The places where the towns grew were close to Roman forts. The language of Britain became English which still has many words from the Roman times. The English word for a 'seller' is a *vendor,* in Roman it would be *venditio, vente* in French, and *vende* in Spanish.

Word Bank

Equites	engineers
armour	Secutor
arena	successful
favourite	country
Thracians	colonies
Colosseum	Britain
aqueducts	soldiers
gladiators	buildings
empire	fighting
powerful	emperor
questions	prisoners
fiercely	Retiarius